7217 ~ Inspired Joy

Sariah Ellsmore

© 2020 by Sariah Ellsmore

All rights reserved. No part of this book may be reproduced or used in any manner with out written permission from the author, except for the use of quotation in the book review.

Library of Congress Cataloging-in-Publication Data

Ellsmore, Sariah.

Print ISBN: 978-1-944066-33-8

Printed in the United States of America

1 2 3 4 5 6 7 8 9 10

Contents

Introduction	7
Chapter 1 Check In	11
Chapter 2 Life~	15
Chapter 3 Perspective	25
Chapter 4 Beliefs	35
Chapter 5 The Self	45
Chapter 6 Creativity	53
Chapter 7 Learning and Teaching	58
Chapter 8 Work/Play/Fun	63
Chapter 9 SEX	76
Chapter 10 Contrast	80
Chapter 11 Pack Your Bags	85
Chapter 12 Meditation	91
Excerpt from *Sunn*	105
Excerpt from *Year Two*	107
Author's Bio	109

Chapter 1
Check In

When life gives you lemons…cut those damn lemons open, suck out the juice, drink down the sour acid then plant the seeds in the earth and watch as a new, beautiful forest of lemon trees blossoms.

I'm in Florida. I moved from my beautiful mountain town of Pagosa Springs, Colorado, just a few months ago. Halloween just happened, and the final quarter of this strange year is coming to an end. 2020 is the year of COVID-19, solitude, social distancing, masks and fear. For me, this has also been a year of finding and enjoying a loving companion, venturing out into nature, home workouts and lots of art.

I am writing the completion of this, my third book, which I have been working on for the entire year. Writing for me is a daily process, and since my daughter died, it has given me a place of solace.

It has been 1050 days since Juliana left this world. For almost three full years, I've wandered around aimlessly, like a chicken with her head cut off.

Searching for comfort and peace of mind has been a tricky path, especially while navigating with a broken heart.

This journey has inspired many beautiful findings in my life, from a firsthand experience of walking my talk I share with you.

As I'm writing these words, I look across the room I'm staying in and see a beautiful teapot that holds my daughters' ashes.

Her death has brought about an absolute knowing that life is temporary. My life is temporary. The things I am going through are also temporary. Pain, grief, sadness, loneliness, frustration, and confusion will eventually subside, and what is left is glorious.

Living is a fantastic game of feeling. Feeling every ounce of emotion that bubbles up has allowed me to develop a new connection and appreciation for my own heart.

I feel a bold awareness that can only come from moving through pain then letting it go.

I'm letting it go.

I'm letting the story of sadness go. I'm letting the death go. I'm letting her go.

Letting go isn't about forgetting; rather, it's about remembering in a way that can serve as a great inspiration.

I imagine it's like holding tightly onto a butterfly then deciding to open my hand, letting the butterfly spread its wings, all the while having a view of its delicate beauty as it gracefully flies away.

The releasing of the butterfly is a relaxing and accepting and opening. It's the surrendering to the moment and appreciating its beauty.

I know in the deepest part of my being that I will see her again, and I can let her go now. I know she would never want me to hold onto sadness or pain. I know she would want me to live a full and meaningful life. I know one day I too will go. In the meantime, I want to take this game and rock it. Play like a pro. I want to win at creating, loving, and sharing.

I have learned many little tricks along this path, different ways to view my life and allow for perspective to permeate the seams. These tips may or may not resonate with you at this time; however, it is my intention to share in hopes that maybe, just *maybe*, I can help you navigate your life into a beautiful creation—a life full of fun and love and appreciation.

I hope to inspire you to look deeply at your time on this planet and to choose to live the most glorious version of yourself imaginable.

As Stephen King wrote in *Shawshank Redemption*, *"It's time to get busy living or get busy dying."*

It's time.

Chapter 2
Life~

What is it anyway?

It seems like we are born, we have a handful of years then we die.

Two important dates are our birthday and our death day. They are separated by a dash that represents our entire life. There is a beautiful poem by Linda Ellis called *The Dash*. It's an inspiring look at how we spend that dash.

How are you spending the dash?

I woke one night at 3am with a thought about our individual paths, and how we are all on the same path but placed at different junctures. My daughter was so much further ahead on her path than I am even at this point. I've been on my path 47 years; her entire life path lasted 7,217 days. Her short dash has inspired me to pay attention, to notice what I notice, to love myself, to share love, to be kind and most of all to enjoy the ups and downs of the fantastic ride.

How many days have you been on your path?

How many more do you think you have?

Paying Attention

It seems easy enough. However, this is one concept that has been tricky for me. It's so easy to wander off mentally and emotionally, to detach from everything around me or to numb myself from what is happening in the moment.

My first true lesson in paying attention happened right after my daughter died. I was in such a state of despair that I needed signs in order to get through my day. Sure enough, she was bringing me all kinds of signs. We had decided before her death that our symbol, if either of us should die before the other, would be diamonds.

Two days after she passed, I started receiving diamonds. Everywhere I looked were diamonds. I still get diamonds occasionally and feel so tremendously grateful each time I receive this special message.

Our loved ones do everything they can to communicate with us after they pass. They want us to know they are still here, just without bodies. They marvel in our lives; they share love and comfort. It's up to us to pay attention.

As time passed, I started taking more and more time for myself, sitting quietly in the hopes that I would be able to get clearer communication. What I found from all this quiet time was I still have so many things in my life that I wish to experience. I realized that my journey was just beginning, and it was time for me to live fully. All the little things that used to frustrate me started to vanish. I began moving through my day calmly, with awareness. I had a deep desire to pay attention to all of life around me and within me. I noticed that by swallowing this giant chill-pill, the world around me started to feel calm. I noticed there was nothing too serious, including myself. The world was shifting because I was shifting.

It's kind of like setting the cruise control on your vehicle. I set the cruise, turned up the music then allowed the journey to unfold all while holding the desire to pay attention.

The first step to living a more powerful and delightful life is to pay attention. How do we do this?

It's really simple.

Slow down!

Stop taking yourself so seriously.

Open your eyes and discover what is holding you back.

See your own magnificence, and you will see it in others.

Be kind. Everyone is on their own rocky path, and we never can really know why someone is acting the way they are acting. If we allow each person to have their stuff, and do not take it personally, we can move from uncomfortable situations, let them go, and get busy attending to our own unfolding.

Now the really important subject: you.

Who are you?

How did you get here?

Better question, why are you here?

Our Creation

How did we get here, and why did we come in the first place?

Stories are a useful tool when trying to make sense of the world. Our lives are filled with many powerful stories. Most of them are made up. It doesn't really matter which story you choose to believe. It is more about the impact the story holds that gives it meaning and purpose. This is a story I like to share, simply because it allows for me to believe in a source and in my connection to it. Source is the beginning and the end and everything in between; we are made up of source. This means we are all the same. We are all connected.

A different story of creation~

There once was a being so magnificent and expansive. This being was everything we can imagine: all the stars, all the planets, all the people and animals and plants. This being was all the ideas and imaginations and love in the entire known and unknown universe. This being was all the space and all the matter. This being wanted to know itself.

As we all know, it's impossible to know what or who we are without some sort of reflection. We need an outside perspective to get a peek into what and who we are. It's impossible to get an outside perspective when we are both inside and outside. It's impossible to know the nature of anything unless there is some sort of contrast.

This being decided to play a game with itself, and it exploded into a billion trillion zillion tiny pieces. The game was about forgetting; each speck of this magnanimous being had to forget that it was and is originally apart of the whole being.

Each speck expanded outward to create the planets and solar systems and the microscopic life forms filling all matter.

Each speck had a purpose, it was to know itself.

As the specks started bumping into other specks, they were all able to decipher their separateness, feel their own boundaries and create a story of the other.

This game was to continue in order to expand the original being. This game was to continue until each tiny speck finally understood its origin and one by one came back to the whole.

We are the specks.

You and I are a part of something vast and glorious. Our tiny human brains cannot comprehend the trueness of our magnificence, so we play out a game of limitation and separateness.

The story you believe about your creation is really not important, but the things you choose to believe will most definitely create the world of your experience.

Understanding there is a purpose for your existence is a great place to start in creating a life you love.

Who you are is love.

Why you are here is to remember who you are.

The purpose of your life is to expand. The direct result of this expansion is joy.

Happiness

We are here to be happy

Happy has many faces. The word itself is simply a description for a state of being. That state of being can also be described as joy, love, presence, inspiration, connection, source, beauty, truth, wisdom, wholeness, enlightenment, etc. For the sake of this conversation, *happy* is the word I'm choosing to use.

At the very core of everything you are and ever will be is happiness.

You are happy; you just forgot. Being here on this planet in this body with these struggles has given you a deep desire to remember.

This is why you are here—to remember.

This is why all of us are here in our little lives running in endless circles. We all know deep down inside that there is something more.

It is calling us to experience more of who we really are. Every action at its core boils down to the ultimate search for this illusive happiness. The cosmic joke is that it's already inside each of us.

If you take any action and dissect it, separate all the little reasons. You will find that at the middle of the action is a desire to JUST BE HAPPY.

Happiness is a state of being—it is your state of being—but you must choose to be it before you will ever experience it.

The greatest search will always bring us back to ourselves.

You are perfection and magnificence bottled into a temporary physical experience simply for the purpose of being happy.

All the things you fight for, strive for, work for, and search for ultimately boil down to the desire to experience the real you, the real happiness.

Why is life so challenging?

Simply because we all like a good challenge.

The best stories come from overcoming the greatest obstacles. Our human lives are made op of stories. We all love to win.

In order to truly win at life, we must first remember why we are here in the first place. We are here to be happy, and happy is already you. The answer to the great question is *you*.

In order to win at life, you must be happy.

The world we live in is dual in nature, yin and yang, light and dark. If one experience is possible, then so is its opposite. When we find ourselves in a dark and challenging place, know that the flip side of the experience is its exact opposite. If you are capable of feeling one of the sides, you are equally capable of feeling its opposite.

The darkest, coldest part of the night always happens before the rising sun. The dawn will come. It has to; it's part of the nature of this world.

The dawn is coming. You are the rising sun.

You are bringing yourself to the party, and now its spectacular.

When you choose to show up being your true self, being happiness, you are the dawn.

The game we came here to play is about creation. It is the reason for this world. We all came here to create all kinds of things and experiences.

When we create from our deepest, truest part of our selves (happiness), our creations reflect that spender. In the process of creating, we get to experience more of who we really are.

You and I and every other being in this entire bubble of existence are the same, we are all the answer, we are all happiness.

Recap:

Remember who you are (happiness).

Know your obstacles (opposition).

Know your game (creation).

Win.

Chapter 3
Perspective

"When you change the way you look at things, the things you look at change."

Wayne Dyer

Perspective

How you view the world and your life in it creates the world of your experience.

The way we view our lives is a combination of the mental programs we have been taught along with the beliefs we hold about ourselves and the world around us.

A good way to think about perspective is this: imagine looking at a painting really close up. All the specs of color and light and dark look like a jumbled chaotic mess. If you step back a few feet, the picture will start to come into view, and you will see the connection of the dots of color and shadow. Images will begin to form. Take a few more steps back and those images will make sense.

Your life is the same. When you are in the middle of living, it's easy to get caught up in the chaos and struggles of the day to day. It's easy to forget who you are and why you are here when you are busy dealing with deadlines and pressures.

In these moments, it is so important to take a step back and to see what is really going on from a place of observing the big picture.

Changing your perspective can be as simples as going outside, talking to a friend, stretching, taking a five-minute nap, closing your eyes and letting yourself feel relaxed. Flip upside down or stand on a stool. Try holding your breath or putting ice on your face.

Before you get back into the grind make a conscious effort to see your life from a different angle.

Pretend you are a complete stranger looking in. What would that person see?

Different Ways to Change Perspective

If you were to give your life a tag line or a theme, what would it be?

In my case, I said that life was an adventure, and I am a joyful explorer.

Now I think that life is a game, and I am a brilliant player.

When life is a dance, we learn how to gracefully move with it.

When life is a struggle, our experiences are hard to move through.

If life were a party, than we would be here to float around and mingle and have fun.

If life is a battle, then we would have to always be fighting.

The way you view life will directly influence the life that shows up for you.

"If you want something you have never had, you have to be willing to do something you have never done."
Thomas Jefferson

Get Curious, Ask Questions, Wonder

By wondering, we allow ourselves to get curious about a topic in a playful way. By being playful, and not so serious, we allow ourselves to view things with a perspective that uses imagination rather than cold hard facts.

The only way to experience something new is to think something new, and how do we get to the new thought? By first being curious.

Being, thinking, doing, and experiencing equals expansion, which allows us to feel joy.

You can practice curiosity right now by wondering about anything. Take a pencil, for example. If think about a pencil, get curious about it; maybe hold it in your hand. You will notice the weight, size, and shape. The next question you may ask yourself is, who designed it in the first place? How did they get the lead to stay within the wood? You'll notice that something so simple that we take completely for granted at one point in time was once someone else's curiosity and obsession and creation.

Nowadays, it's easy to find many of the answers by using Google's search engine; however, if you give your brain the permission, it can conjure up many wonderful questions, which will inspire the use of your imagination.

One story I like to refer to is in my second book, *Year Two*.

I talk about a time when my daughter was feeling down and lost. She wanted to be inspired but didn't know where to start. I challenged her to imagine she was a tiger trainer. I told her to get curious and play around with the idea for a while and to think about all the things she would have to do in order to be a tiger trainer. Where would she have to go to school? Where would she live and work? I challenged her to take a little trip in her imagination and to see where it would lead.

Later, after she died, I had an experience of feeling lost. I was sitting in my shower crying, and I heard out loud, "What if you decided to be a tiger trainer?"

She was inspiring me to get curious and to wonder myself into a new reality.

Notice What You Notice

When we make the commitment to pay attention, we begin to view a new larger perspective of our lives and notice what we notice.

Notice the habitual thoughts that run rampant; notice the words you speak out loud; notice the perpetual feelings that come with the words.

By noticing what you notice, you will be able to catch yourself when you are in the middle of an old way of being and shift it to something else.

I especially like to use this practice any time I'm in a new place or situation. When showing up to a party or meeting or when traveling alone, I like to pay attention to what catches my awareness. I notice what I notice. At most times, I carry around a journal and write down notes.

For instance, as I walked into a bookstore the other day, I noticed all the people walking around not looking at each other. I noticed different body types, sizes and shapes. I noticed that I was drawn to a private corner where I could set up and have a good view of all the people walking around. I noticed the barista behind the coffee counter was jacked up on caffeine.

Traveling alone in an airport, I noticed body alignment. I noticed how people were walking. I noticed that my own walk was much faster. I noticed that I was feeling insecure and wanted to appear to have a place to walk to. I noticed a strange electric feeling in the air; it felt like buzzing bees and lots of energy moving around. I also noticed I loved listening to foreign languages being spoken.

We will all notice different things according to the filters we have set on our mind. In my case, I have always been fascinated with the human form, and I've learned a lot about alignment through different avenues of training, such as massage school and yoga teacher training as well as CrossFit coaching and dance. I look at the body as a work of art, and I appreciate the many varieties.

An interior decorator may notice the design in a room and the placement of chairs and tables or the color scheme. An electrician may notice the light sockets and outlets; they would notice if a wire was out of place.

A comedian would notice all the things that are funny with a situation. A mother would probably notice all the little kids.

An angry person may notice more reasons to be angry. Someone who is sad would see more reasons to be sad.

I use this practice to learn more about myself and about the automatic thoughts I tend to have.

By noticing what we notice, we can begin to see the program that is running us. Once we notice, we can choose if it is something that serves our growth or not.

Creating a Time Line (The Playing Field of Your Life)

Take a few moments to write out the life you have already lived. Start with your early family and continue on through the experiences you remember. Give as much detail as you can think of. Write down the feelings, emotions and beliefs tied to each event. Notice when you said something at one time and then at a later date it happened. Notice how people came into your life exactly at the right time and left when you were ready to move on. Notice the things you went through felt sometimes so unbearable and at a later time you found that those moments were great gifts of learning.

In all this investigating, you will start to see a theme tying all the different stories together. You will start to see an underlying program and a belief system. As you view these events, do so without critical judgement. All these events are the reason you are the way you are and the combination of all the questions, struggles, mishaps and moments you feel proud of; they created the person you are today. This desire to know yourself better is a perfect playing field for creating a life you love.

My Own Personal Timeline

As a young person, I was raised with a very strict set of beliefs. The religion I was born into didn't leave much room for questions or thinking for myself. My childhood was simple enough, safe enough, and dull enough to inspire a great desire to open to the world and to question everything. I was raised as a Mormon with 11 siblings; my parents moved our family every year to a new place. I had a very unique programmed understanding of the world. Within this early experience, I learned that life would turn out, even if it seemed unlikely.

I remember living in Mexico as illegal aliens while my father traveled for work. Having no food to eat, I climbed fruit trees to feed my siblings. I learned to sew my own clothes at a young age and also became the family barber. (To this day, I still enjoy sewing and cutting hair.) I learned how to be resourceful and cook with limited ingredients.

I left my family at 17; I decided to do whatever it took to get an education and a life of my own. I attended Utah State University with the help of government funding, and I was able to study and learn. I fell in love with learning. I dropped out of collage when I met my husband at 20. Together we created 4 beautiful babies and a thriving business, which afforded us the luxury of buying property and building a gorgeous home in Colorado. Twenty-three years later, all the kids had grown, and my husband and I decided to divorce. Eight months after the separation, we lost one of our daughters. She died in a car accident; we think she fell asleep at the wheel and drove off a cliff.

This is where the story begins. This one accident, this one single event, this moment in time that supersedes all the moments in time has created such an impact that life's very makeup has exploded into a billion tiny pieces and the clean-up process is the very reason why I write.

The early part of my life was the set-up, a stage and a story that would create the contrast for my own desire to learn. The latter part was a catalyst; it was the emotional boost I needed in order to put the things I had been learning into play. The explosion of my life was an opportunity to view all the little pieces of my life and to evaluate the importance then reassemble in a way that I wanted. It was a great undoing followed by a great creation of my choosing—kind of like the phoenix rising from the ashes.

The next part of this exercise is to create an imaginary timeline backwards. Start at your death and write down all the things you imagine yourself creating. Get extravagant with this exercise; after all, it is only your imagination.

"Shoot for the moon. Even if you miss, you'll land among the stars."

Norman Vincent Peale

"Life isn't about finding yourself; it's about creating yourself."

George Bernard Shaw

Chapter 4
Beliefs

Understanding Your Belief System (The Program)

Beliefs are the mental program you live by. They are like a pair of glasses with different colored lenses. If you wear them long enough, everything you see will be tinted by the lens color. The world you see will be a little different from the world other people see, simply because we each have different colored lenses in our glasses.

Your beliefs create your reality.

What you believe about yourself, your world, your relationships and even your God all set the stage of your life saga.

Beliefs are just the thoughts you think all the time.

What are your beliefs?

How can we get to the middle of it?

This has been a question I sit with often. I have always been curious about the mental program running the show.

In my own personal life, early on I was programmed to believe in a heaven and hell and an unforgiving creator who watched every move I made, judging my actions and choices along the way. I was afraid to make a mistake or step out of line. I was afraid of trying new things or even thinking differently than I was taught. This program was really solid. I felt constrained and wanted to break out of the tiny box of my life. I think this is a natural stage for most of us. We are born into one way of thinking, but somehow, we know there is more, and we want to break free and choose for ourselves.

This happened early on for me. I was 17 when I decided I would choose my own beliefs. I started questioning everything.

By taking the time to evaluate my own beliefs, I was able to change them.

Now I choose to believe differently.

I believe that we are all connected, and the things we choose are simply the things we choose. The consequences play out nicely for most of our choices in this life. There isn't a father figure waiting to punish us for mistakes. In fact, the mistakes are all a part of the big picture. The mistakes are the contrast we were seeking in order to know ourselves more intimately. We choose and then choose again, hopefully making better and better choices along the way.

Knowing that you can change your beliefs is a powerful way to begin to choose your way into a new and fulfilling life design of your own creation.

This is a practice in changing the very program that runs you.

Choose to believe only the things that serve to continue the growth and expansion of your being.

Honesty (Fearless Responsibility)

Being honest with yourself about who you are and what you want in life is one of the most courageous things you can do for yourself. After all, it is your life experience; you are the one who has to live it. Taking absolute responsibility for who you are and letting go of blame is a bold place to stand. Choosing to live a powerful life full of fun and adventure can only come from first being completely honest with yourself.

This doesn't mean inflicting your opinion on anyone, but rather respecting that every person has their own life to live, and they get to choose for themselves.

"The truth will set you free" isn't just a nice saying; it's a reality. Your truth will set you free. By courageously claiming your truth, you are also accepting that others may not agree with you and that it is ok to let the cards fall where they may. This life is about you remembering that you are here to live the best life you can imagine for yourself.

It took me many years to learn this lesson. I lived decades not being completely honest with myself, blaming others for why I was feeling the way I was feeling, or blaming them for my own setbacks. I would look outside myself and point fingers, making everything I was experiencing about the people and circumstances in my life. The only problem with living this way is it's not very fun. In fact, it's the opposite of fun. It feels more like living in a deep cave with no sunlight. By blaming others, I was giving them my power. I felt powerless and trapped.

Being a powerful creator is the most fun you can ever have in this life. The only way to access your own personal power is to be honest.

Fear

> "The cave you fear to enter holds
> the treasure that you seek."
>
> Joseph Campbell

What is fear?

Why are we so infested with it?

What is the opposite of fear?

How do we access that?

False Evidence Appearing Real

Fear is a part of being human; it is a program imprinted deeply in our DNA. It was placed there as a security measure. It is a program that kept us alive when we had predators. It is a measuring barometer that helps us to be cautious and move deliberately through our day. However, much of the fear we experience is not real.

I love the quote by Will Smith in his movie *After Earth* when talking to his son about fear:

> "The only place that fear can exist is in our thoughts of the future. It is a product of our imagination, causing us to fear things that do not at present and may not ever exist. That is near insanity, Kitai. Do not misunderstand me, danger is very real, but fear is a choice."
>
> Will Smith –*After Earth*

What does a life without fear look like? It looks like *trust*. It is trusting there is a purpose to our existence and knowing things will work out. It is having a great appreciation for the time we are here and knowing that our time here will come to an end. Every person will end. In the meantime, putting fear in check will allow for an exciting curiosity to bubble up and push you into circumstances that otherwise may not be available to you. It is saying yes to life and moving boldly into the unknown.

See It as You Wish It to Be

This is one of my favorite ways to counter the feelings of fear.

For many years, I would wake up in the middle of the night sweating, heart racing, with thoughts of all the things that could go wrong in my life. I would worry about my children. I would think about my husband leaving me. I would obsess over money and the lack of it. I would see disasters and fear they were headed for me. I was sure my house was going to burn down, or my kids would die, or the IRS would come and take everything away from us. I would think about being homeless. I would think about my car breaking down.

Funny sidenote: now that I'm writing these things down, I realize I've actually experienced many of these things first hand.

The actual experiences were nothing like the fear of the experiences.

When bad things showed up, I found I was able to move through them with graceful resolve. (I do question if my obsession and fear actually brought these experiences into my life.)

The practice of "seeing it as I wish it to be" seems a little outlandish at first, but when you get in to the habit of changing your mind at the onset of the fearful thought, you will find that the fear will dissipate, and your experiences will shift to more positive manifestations of your own creation.

How to do it?

When you find yourself in the middle of a fantasy of worry, stress, and fear, STOP yourself immediately. Remind yourself that the stories running rampant are your imagination, and since it is your imagination, you can control it. You can imagine differently.

Take a few moments to imagine the greatest possible scenario. Allow yourself to see it in vivid color and texture. Allow yourself to feel how amazing the new imagination feels, and obsess about that. The wonderful part about this whole practice is knowing that imagination is the source of creation. Imagination and belief work hand in hand. You imagine first and believe second.

Believe that the lovely things you want to experience are coming; they are on their way right now. Remember, this life is a fantastic game of creation, and we create the realities we experience. Using your mind to imagine and your heart to believe will allow for these things to show up in splendor.

Time

"Don't waste your time or time will waste you."
Muse , Knights of Cydonia

"The only reason for time is so that everything doesn't happen at once.".
Albert Einstein

You Still Have Time

Time is a tricky thing. It seems that when we are having fun, there isn't enough of it. When we are doing something we hate, there is way too much of it.

Albert Einstein argued that time is an illusion. I love his quote: *"When you sit with a nice girl for two hours, it feels like two minutes; when you sit on a hot stove for two minutes, it feels like two hours. That's relativity."*

How many times have you heard or even said, "I would love to do that, but I don't have time"?

If you wake up and find yourself breathing in a body, then you have time.

Time is given to us generously by life. Being alive means we have time.

However, time is something we must take from life.

The key to making the most of time is to live as if time were unlimited.

Having an appreciation for the minutes and seconds that present themselves to you will make them appreciate.

I have found that the trick to time is to fill it with intention.

If you intend on taking your time, enjoying the ride, and moving with ease, you'll find that time works with you.

If you have a habit of rushing, then time will feel like a rush.

If you complain about not having time, then your experience of time will be exactly that.

An adorable elderly fellow gave me the best advice I have ever heard. One day he was 40 then the next day he was 77; it all happened so fast. He blinked, and time dissolved. "Do not blink."

He lives an amazing life now of not blinking but it came with the great price of 37 lost years.

When my daughter died, I struggled with time, regretting the time I would not have with her and feeling the sadness and loss around her short 19 years on the planet.

Her death is the reason I appreciate my time now. I appreciate the time I have with my living children. I appreciate the time I get to spend with those I love. I even appreciate the time spent doing things that are not so pleasant, knowing that I get to learn and grow from those moments.

In the end our entire timeline will be whittled down into a handful of moments, experiences and memories.

What we choose to do with our precious time is up to us. Do not blink.

Chapter 5
The Self

Self-Love

It doesn't matter what you do; it matters what you think about what you do.

If you type in the words "self-love" on your computer, thousands upon thousands of results will appear. Apparently, this is a huge topic for all of us on this planet.

Why?

Why is loving ourselves so hard?

What does it even look like?

How does a life of self-love actually make any difference in our lives?

Let's dissect this just a little bit.

If you could wave a magic wand and one day wake up with so much love and adoration for the person in the mirror, how would you feel?

Imagine all the little criticisms and doubts just vanished. You would suddenly be your biggest fan. You would have so much energy available to do the things you always dreamed about. You would allow yourself to dress as you feel, and walk tall. Your face would smile, and your heart would sing. Life would feel so wonderful, and you would have a tremendous appreciation for the body you are in. You would know your worth and beauty. You would see those qualities in every person who crossed your path.

Doors would open for you and opportunities would flow to you.

We are all programmed from the very beginning of our lives. The first people who love us and teach us also program us. We see the world from their view and adopt their way of thinking. As we grow, this group of influential programmers grows to be our teachers, our friends, the communities we belong to, and the religions and cultures we are surrounded by. Sometimes, those views can be constructive, but many times, they can be limiting and destructive.

Every being is born perfect.

The training to be human is where the neuroses set in. There are so many pressures to be something other than what and who you already are. Most people find that they secretly hate themselves (just ask any teenage girl). Why are we so unhappy?

Somewhere in the middle of our human programmed mind, there is an ideal, a standard set. It's a picture of the perfect unattainable us that is more beautiful, smarter, funnier, and richer. We believe there's a healthier, happier version of us, and the things we are doing will never let us get to this fictitious place. The crazy part is we all know it; we may not admit it but every one of us is guilty. We want something different than what we already have, believing that we will be so much better off if only (fill in the blank).

I had a teacher once tell me that "nothing will make me happy." I remember thinking, what an idiot, how can he say that? Surely if I just had a better body and more money, then I would be the happiest person on the planet. Well, I got a better body and more money and guess what—I wasn't any happier. In fact, the exact opposite happened. I was more discouraged because I thought the things I was seeking were the answers, and when I was proven wrong, I felt like I had to start all over.

We already have everything we need to be happy right now in this very moment.

Happiness isn't something to be found; it's something to be lived. It's a choice in the moment.

It comes from a complete and total acceptance and love of ourselves (warts and all).

The way to this happy land is to stop hating and start loving. Love it all—the wrinkles, the blemishes, the bad relationships, and the shitty jobs. Love the height, the weight, the eye color, the skin. Love the heart and the mind. Love the family and the upbringing. Love the struggles, love the defeats.

Every person struggles with something; we all have this in common, but the way to enjoy it is to choose to love it.

Suffering comes from a need to be experiencing something other than what you are experiencing. Rather than suffer, love the struggle.

Here is the story of how I got the better body:

After having four babies stretch and expand my body, I felt very insecure about the excess weight and stretch marks, not to mention my diminished boobs. There was nothing left but sad bags of skin. I was so mean to myself every time I looked in the mirror. I face smile? Can I see myself enjoying the situation with a buoyant heart? Does the situation make my body tense?

Our bodies are amazing barometers; they are so incredibly sensitive and intelligent. Getting connected to the subtle sensations the body offers is getting connected to intuition. I used to think that I needed an answer by hearing a voice, but I have since learned that my feelings are the answer.

Take time to observe your own unique body and learn what it is communicating to you.

A fantastic book by Louise Hay, *You Can Heal Your Life,* is a great resource for understanding the intelligence of the body and how different thoughts affect our wellbeing.

We all have the ability to tap into intuition, by setting the intention to pay attention and by believing it is possible, intuition will show up for us.

Sometimes, promptings will come as a whisper or maybe as a picture you see in your mind, a gut feeling or simply a deep desire to turn in a particular direction. All this is connection to intuition and to your own unique psychic abilities. When they are accompanied with feeling good, then it's an indicator that it is the right thing for you.

When I find myself getting caught up in the swirling fantasies of my mind, I have a tendency to ignore my body. When I ignore my body, I feel disconnected from the physical world.

We are here to be in our bodies, not to escape them. That part comes later. The body is the access to sensation, and sensation is access to the present moment.

Moving with Intuition

We are all born with a unique set of abilities and talents, many of which need to be developed. One of those abilities is intuition. It is the process of tapping into your higher, much wiser self. This part of you is always present, but it's up to you to connect with it.

I have learned to tap into my own intuition by first getting quiet. I sit with myself, focus on my breath for a few moments, relax my body, and ask my question. I simply ask myself if the choice I'm making is the right choice, and then I listen and feel. I use the sensations in my body to determine if what I am wanting is right for me.

For instance, if I have been invited to do something, I will first imagine myself in that situation and notice how my body reacts. How does the situation feel? Does my stomach feel tight? Do my lungs feel full? Does my cultivate a more loving and accepting view. When you appreciate something, it raises the value. Appreciating the being you are and the life you have is a great start. It only gets better!

Your Body Is Here to Be Used

Our bodies are magnificent; we are inside them to use them as a vehicle of experience. It is through our bodies that we get to use sensation to feel our present moment.

When we feel disconnected from the body, it is simply because we are not being present. The way back to the present moment is through our bodies. Feeling the sensation of the moment will bring our awareness into the moment.

If you stop right now and ask, what am I seeing? What am I hearing, smelling, tasting? What does my skin feel? Noticing your sensations will give you direct access to the infamous NOW.

There is so much talk around being in the moment but little explanation as to how to access it.

I asked, I've been asking, and in the asking, I'm given a quiet little nudge to use my body as a doorway to the experience of NOW.

would say the nastiest things about my poor body. I was disgusted. Even though I worked out every day and ate very healthy, I still struggled with my appearance. Then one day out of the blue, I caught myself being rude to the image I saw in the mirror. I realized I would never say any of these mean things to any person on the planet. Why was I saying them to myself? I decided then and there that I would not say another unkind word about the body that made the lives of my beautiful babies possible. Instead, I stared deeply in the mirror and said thank you. I thanked my skin, I thanked my limbs, I thanked my heart and my mind and my face and my eyes. I made a bath and lit candles and proceeded to thank and love every inch of this human form, promising to never betray her again. I promised to only see the beauty.

What happened next was a miracle: my body responded. She lost the weight, the skin tightened back up, my hair became thicker and my boobs returned.

What I learned was what I was doing wasn't the important part; it was what I thought about what I was doing that made the difference.

Knowing that we are here to grow and expand, it would make sense to pay attention to the thoughts we have about ourselves and to see where we can

Chapter 6
Creativity

How do I access creativity?

By being creative.

How can I be creative if I've never been creative?

Get curious about it, start asking questions, use your imagination. Get interested in others who have created. Imagine you are living inside of their mind. What would it look like? What would it feel like? How would you see the world?

Then allow. Allowing is the opposite of resisting. Let your guard down, let your judgements go. Let expectation go. Simply create from the core of your being.

Be creative.

We Are Here to Create

One of the best things about living is we are walking, talking creators. We create in every moment, whether we are aware of it or not. When we understand how it happens, then we create from a place of awareness and deliberation. Being creators is our birthright. Creating on purpose brings pure joy with it.

Accessing Imagination

Imagination is the beginning point of all creation. Imagination and belief go hand in hand. If you can imagine it, then you can create it.

I love this thought, and I love paying attention to my imagination. I also use my dream state to access this realm.

I had a dream recently about a solar-powered generator that was light enough to power a helicopter. In my dream, Elon Musk and I made a beautiful lightweight energy-efficient helicopter together. Great dream, right? Well, as technology advances, who knows—maybe the day will come when I can have a little sit-down with Elon.

Allowing for imagination is allowing for our minds to be open to possibilities. When these possibilities pop up, rather than discount them, use them. Let these ideas float around you and inspire even more creative ideas. Once you start, you are going to find you are a creative master being, and you will be able to look at all the happenings in your life and draw inspiration.

Meditation

Meditation is the act of sitting quietly and allowing for your mind and body and spirit to connect without any effort. It's a sort of reset and a doorway to remembering who you are and why you are here. I use meditation all the time. I have included a handful of personal meditation practices in the final chapter of this book. Learning to get quiet and just be allows for access into the very core of our being, and in this core is the cumulation of all the imagination and creation that ever was or ever will be. This is a very powerful place to visit. It's definitely worth trying.

Talent Is a Beautiful Thing

Being generous with our talents and sharing them is our own personal gift to the world. Being afraid or insecure or even denying the talent all together is a tragedy. Your talent is a unique expression of you. It can be anything from giving foot rubs to cooking, singing even organizing.

A clue to understanding your talent when you are in the middle of doing something is to notice how it makes you feel. If you experience feelings of lightness, joy, pleasure, and even time loss, this could be an indicator that you possess a talent for whatever it is you are doing.

The secret is to pay attention to how you feel while doing something. The next step is to allow yourself to develop these talents. Get really good at them. Having a playful attitude towards your practice allows you to develop without the pressure of needing to be perfect. Just have fun. Judging your abilities is the quickest way to squash your talents, so let judgment go.

You don't have to be great to enjoy what you're doing, but you do have to enjoy what you're doing in order to be great.

For most of my life, I thought I was really bad at painting. Just a few months ago, my son and daughter were visiting. He suggested we pick up some canvases and paint. My first response was, "That's not going to be any fun. I suck at painting." He encouraged me to just let go of my judgment and to try it anyway. I decided to give it a go. Together, we all sat around the table and listened to music; we talked and laughed. I thought about how much I love my kids and enjoy spending time with them. I ended up painting a gorgeous sea turtle effortlessly. I wasn't thinking about how bad I was, but instead, I was focused on enjoying my time with my kids. Being in a state of love and sharing allowed for my critical brain to shut off and for my talent for painting to turn on. I surprised myself. I had no idea that I would enjoy this form of expression so much. Since that night, I have been playing with paint on a consistent basis and have actually been hired to create art. Now when I paint, I lose track of time; it's as if I become part of the colors and feel my way around the images from a deep part of myself. I become the painting.

Share your talents and share your creations; they are your gifts to the world.

> "Don't die with your music still in you."
> Wayne Dyer

Chapter 7
Learning and Teaching

"The only things we get to keep are
the things we give away."

Bill Vaughan

"You can have everything in life you want, if you will just
help enough other people get what they want."

Zig Ziglar

We Teach What We Need to Learn

Learning to navigate my own life of uncertainty, I decided to view all my personal challenges as college courses. I am here to learn. By sharing and teaching, I am able to better understand the true purpose behind my own obstacles.

I have used this approach throughout most of my life and have found it so useful at this time. Many days feel like I'm running uphill barefoot in a snowstorm. It is during these times I remind myself to look back at my notes and use the things I have already learned to shift the struggle. By sharing with you, I will better remember these concepts. Little by little, I get to be the painter of my own paradise right here. Right now.

It's such an interesting concept to understand that all the things that I struggle with will eventually be the things I become brilliant at.

I deeply want to live from a place of pure joy, yet I find myself in moments that are not joyful. By practicing the things I am teaching, I get to use my life as a first-hand example. By using my own techniques to shift my own perspective and live a fuller, happier life, I get to pass on these concepts to you and hopefully to many generations to follow. Words can change the world.

Always Be Learning-

> "Once you stop learning, you start dying."
> Albert Einstein

There is something to learn from every situation, every person, every moment. When we look at the world through the lens of learning, then we can open up to the mystery hidden in the crevices of life.

When we find ourselves in situations that are just so tough, we must remember there is always something to learn. Mistakes will happen; they are part of being human. Mishaps, setbacks, bad choices and even bad relationships are all opportunities to learn and grow. This is why we are here.

When something happens that is just so wrong, look again; there is clearly something to learn. Learning about the things you don't like or the things you will never do again is a tremendous lesson—probably the best lesson a person can learn. Remember you can always choose better.

Rather than beat yourself up about something that has happened, see if maybe there might be a greater perspective and learn from it.

"Live as if you were to die tomorrow; learn as if you were to live forever."

Mahatma Gandhi

Try Something New

Why is it that we tend to limit ourselves when it comes to trying something new? We start off by saying, "I could never do (fill in the blank)."

How can we say that if we have never tried in the first place?

Using the concept of noticing what you notice, notice when you say limiting things about your abilities when it comes to something new. Who knows, maybe you'll be great at the new thing. You will never know until you give it a solid try.

When I was a little girl, I used to say that I was really clumsy, and I couldn't dance. Now one of my greatest joys in life is aerial art. After many years of practice, I am a graceful dancing aerial artist. I've performed for giant audiences, and I love the thrill of being on stage. Had I continued to believe that I was clumsy, I would have never known the pure ecstasy of dance.

As a young mother, I wanted to go back to school. I valued education but had dropped out of collage to get married. I promised myself that I would continue with my education once my children were in full-time school. At that time, we lived in a place that didn't have a school where I could continue with my philosophy degree. I decided to start over. I randomly chose to become a helicopter pilot. I had no experience with aviation, but something in me wanted to give it a go. Later, I found that flying helicopters would be one of the hardest things I ever tried, but I stuck with it and after many hours of practice and study, I learned to fly like a pro. At the time, that gigantic undertaking made me look at the many areas in my life where I felt insecure. Becoming a pilot brought about such a tremendous sense of confidence and accomplishment, and being able to fly is such a joy.

Instead of the automatic response of "I can't" or "I suck at that," how about saying, "I'll give it a try." Who knows, maybe the next thing you try will fill you with so much joy that you will wonder why you waited so long to try it.

Chapter 8
Work/Play/Fun

Work

I just caught myself saying to my honey, "I'm going to do a little work," meaning I was going to sit down and write.

The concept of work has such strange emotional ties.

Think of how many times we say grudgingly, "I have to go to work,"

or, "all I do is work."

What happens when work is our joy, and the idea of getting to work is a pure expression of delight?

Imagine waking up in the morning so excited to get busy working.

This has been my experience lately. My eyes open, and I feel so much happiness around the work I'm going to create that day. How does this happen?

When we choose to do the things we love, simply because we choose to do them, life lines up for us. That love gets translated into a stream of support, including utility bills and mortgage payments. All our needs will be taken care of.

I've spent many years pondering this concept, and for most of that time, I would laugh doubtingly when someone would say, "When you do what you love, it doesn't feel like work."

I'd like to take it one step deeper. When you bring love into what you are doing, no matter if it's cleaning toilets or bagging groceries, there will be an element of joy and satisfaction in the doing. Time moves more slowly, and we get to experience presence.

The dream job is any job you are presently enjoy.

How do we come to this place?

Mike Dooley explains it very well in his book *Life on Earth*.

He explains that the path to a fulfilling life of creation starts with getting up and moving in the general direction of that dream, by knocking on doors and turning over stones. Eventually, the things we desire will find us because we are willing to move towards them.

This is the process of having the guts to move towards the things we wish to have in our lives.

When we give ourselves permission to have, do, or be something greater than what we are experiencing now, doors will open for us. Opportunities will present themselves. The right people will show up in our lives, and the path will appear.

All this takes great trust. You must trust in yourself and trust that life wants you to be fulfilled in every moment.

I like to think of this process like driving in a storm.

I set my path (allow for my desired destination.)

I drive with awareness looking at the road immediately in front of me.

I pay attention to the present, to the rain, to the cars around me, to the road.

I relax, breathe, turn on the music and let myself focus on the task at hand. I don't worry about the road ahead, knowing that I will be able to take care of whatever may cross my path in that future moment. I also pay no attention to the road behind me. Worrying about the road I have already driven is distracting, and I need to focus on being in the car in the storm. I then do my best to enjoy the drive.

When we change the way we look at work, we realize that it is a privilege to work in the first place. Work becomes a gift. We get to use the work to propel us towards the things we want to experience.

With the right state of mind, work can be so much fun. When you are having fun, life takes on a whole greater meaning. Fun is contagious. When you bring fun to the scene, others will be influenced, and their day will be a little bit brighter because of you.

In the end, it doesn't matter what you do; it simply matters how you do it.

Play

Adding the element of play to any part of your life will immediately give you a feeling of fun, inspiration, and excitement.

Being playful is the opposite of being serious. Having a playful attitude can help you solve serious problems. Being playful is about being open and viewing life with a light heart. Being serious is more rigid, set in stone, hard thinking, which doesn't allow for buoyant, uplifting ideas to permeate your being.

By being playful, you can move through some of life's toughest moments with grace and ease. Playful is contagious and attractive. Like attracts like. Your presence alone will help to shift the mood of those around you, recruiting playmates along the way.

This is an area I struggled with for many years of my life. I didn't know how to play. I felt insecure in my own skin and didn't want to look like a fool. I wanted to be taken seriously. Little did I know that being straight-faced and pretending I was something other than I really was, was more foolish than just enjoying my time and being a happy, playful person. Being serious doesn't make you any smarter; it just makes being around you heavier, dull and cumbersome. No wonder I didn't have many friends at that point.

When we can love ourselves enough and allow ourselves to be happy, play naturally emerges. The element of play enriches your day-to-day experiences and lightens your heart. Playing creates a feeling of buoyancy and an attitude of excitement, acceptance and inclusion.

How do we access play?

The first step is to stop taking yourself so seriously.

Your life is going to happen regardless of how you feel about it. It is short, and one day you will die. You have a choice to either look at the events in your life as a struggle and hardship, letting them weigh you down, or you can change your perspective. See the thread of humor intertwining the irony of our brief time on this planet and move with a smile and a laugh. It all boils down to what you want to experience. I have a sneaky suspicion that if you got this far in the book, then you are wanting to experience play, fun, excitement, creativity, inspiration, joy, etc. It's all up to you.

When my daughter died, and my world exploded, the serious Sariah evaporated in that event. I couldn't take life seriously anymore. This feeling may have come out of a self-preservation necessity, or just out of a feeling that the temporary nature of our lives leaves no room for seriousness. We are only here now, and I want to spend my now enjoying it.

A Couple Ways to Access Play

Shifting Energy

I write about these concepts from a place of actual practice. I use this one all the time. It helps.

When you are feeling down, weird, bored, lonely, sad, or basically any of the emotions that feel horrible, it is possible to shift them.

I have days where everything is going great; I have a happy, positive outlook and a hopeful spirit, but then something happens. It's like a nasty storm blowing in from nowhere.

Sometimes the dark clouds sneak up on me and before I know it, the whole world looks grey.

In my case, this happens sometimes for no reason at all. I just find myself in a shitty mood. The great thing about this is I know that since it is my mood, I am in charge of it, and I can shift it.

My favorite tool is music. I put on happy, upbeat music I love. Sometimes, I just listen, but usually, I end up dancing. The combination of listening to fun music then letting my body move shifts my mood almost immediately.

Today I was feeling down. After sitting with the emotion for a little bit, I realized that there was no real reason behind the mood, so I decided to change it. I turned up the music, grabbed two rags and used them under my feet, which makes the floor slippery and my movements challenging to control. I danced around on the rags, spun in circles, and pretended to be skating. I slid all over the floor giggling. I'm sure if anyone were to look in the windows, they would think I had lost my mind. I looked pretty silly, but that was the point. I wanted to remember to be silly, to be happy and not to take myself so seriously. After about 5 minutes of carrying on, my mood was uplifted. I then sat down and wrote about it.

Whenever I want to write about a specific tool, I notice that the exact thing I am writing about shows up. I get to experience it first-hand, maybe it's just to test it out before I share with you, just to make sure these are valuable lessons and worth sharing.

This world is dual in nature. There is an opposite for everything. Action and reaction, highs and lows, light and dark.

Our emotional states also have opposite emotions.

I like to think of each emotional feeling as if it were a coin; one side of the coin is happiness, and the other side of the coin is sadness. One side is boredom, the other is creativity. Play and seriousness are flip sides of the same coin. When you find yourself stuck in an emotion, it's an opportunity to recognize that the opposite is also available. By learning how to shift, you will have access to the states of emotion you wish to experience.

This comes with practice, but it gets easier and easier the more you practice.

Flip the Script

My younger brother inspired this idea. He had a realization about opposites and wanted to test his theory. As a young man, he hated anything that had to do with country—the music, the dress code. He hated the hats and trucks. One day, he said he wanted to see if he could learn to love what he hated. Sure enough, the next time I saw him, he was driving around a pick-up truck wearing a cowboy hat and listening to country music. When I asked him about his shift, he said he tried it as an experiment but found out that he actually likes being a country boy.

As a young mom, I was always cleaning and cooking and doing laundry—endless piles of dirty clothes. I remember hating every minute of it. I decided to try flipping the script and loving what I hate. I convinced my mind that I actually love doing dishes. If my brother could do it, so could I. Long story short, I actually enjoy doing dishes and almost every place I show up for a visit, you'll find me washing all the dirty dishes in the house.

Remember if you are experiencing one emotion, then its equal and opposite is also available; you just have to want to shift. I recommend making a game out of it. That way, you won't take yourself so seriously. After all, it's just a game, so play it well.

"In Order To" vs "Because I Want To"

The underlying reason to do anything is that somewhere in the doing, we think we will get to experience fun. How many times have you heard or even said, "I just want to have fun. I just want to be happy"? The interesting thing about both of these desires is it doesn't matter what you do; if you are not first experiencing fun and happy, then the doing will not bring them to you.

So many times, we tend to get caught up in the strange mental reasoning of doing things we place "in order to" in front of many of the things we do thinking that one thing will bring us to the other.

For instance, " =I need a relationship in order to not feel lonely," or, "I need to have a great body in order to do the activities I love."

What if we replaced "in order to" with "because I want to"?

What if we were able to own the feelings of desire rather than justifying the desire?

What if you could just say what is really going on and move authentically from that place instead?

This is a tricky place to navigate because so many of us are programmed to believe in a world of cause-and-effect when many of the times the cause and the effect have nothing to do with each other.

The "in order to" is kind of like the middle-man.

It's a side step from the path we really wish to be on.

What if we could avoid the middle-man all together and move directly towards the actual things we wished to experience just because we want to experience them?

Owning our desires is an act of bold courageousness.

Imagine saying what you really want out loud with no reasoning behind it.

I learned this lesson many years ago when I was still married and wanted to go on a yoga retreat just because I wanted to go.

At that time, I was still used to making up reasons to justify my desires. I had to convince myself that if I could make a good argument for my going on the trip, I could justify it to my husband at the time and he would have to let me go.

I told myself that if I used this trip to find peace and solitude, then it would be worth the money I was spending. I came up with a great story about how I never got to be alone and my chaotic life as a mother of four had me frantically searching for peace. This trip would be a reboot, and I would be able to appreciate my life more if I went.

I delivered my argument hoping that my husband would support me completely and see the need for my leaving. What happened next was amazing. He called me out. He said that the story I was telling was a great story, but it wasn't the real reason I wanted to go. He challenged me to just own my desire to just go simply because I wanted to go.

At first, I was offended thinking there was no way I could ever just do something because I wanted to do it. I needed to have many reasons to justify the time I would be away and the money I would be spending.

I learned in that moment to be honest with myself and others. I learned that it's ok to have great desires. I learned that wanting something is enough reason on its own to allow myself to have it.

I would like to challenge you now to own your desires completely. Look at the things you want and let go of the reasoning and justifications. If you want to have fun in your life, start with being fun first. You'll find that fun follows you everywhere; you won't have to go search for it. Happiness is the same. By being happy, you will allow for happiness to be present in any situation. Being playful allows for play to show up.

If you allow yourself to feel content with your own company, loneliness will cease to exist and surprisingly, others will be drawn into your company.

If you allow yourself to do the physical activities you wish to do, your body will respond with a fitness level capable of doing those activities.

If you allow yourself to be friendly, you will find friends everywhere you go.

Being generous allows for generosity to show up in your experience.

Being peaceful first brings a peacefulness into your life.

All the things you wish to have in your life are really about first owning the desire then being that desire simply because you want to.

Chapter 9
SEX

I imagine when the design for humans was being created, there was a lot of humor involved.

The human machine is purely ingenious. These bodies are amazing vehicles that mostly run themselves. All they need is a little food and water, rest and movement, and they can keep walking and talking and figuring things out.

So much of what happens with our vehicles is on autopilot; it just happens because it is the design of the body. Hearts beating, blood pumping, lungs breathing, skin sensing.

Our vehicles come equipped with a fully functioning entertainment system, a pleasure mode—one we can choose to turn ON or OFF at the flip of a switch.

These bodies are the reason we get to experience living on this planet. Every part about your body is useful and important and allows for you to access the sensations that will serve as navigation tools on your journey. One aspect that seems to get overlooked is also the most powerful tool you possess: SEX.

I'm not sure exactly why most of us elect to walk through our lives with our sexy switch set to off. I suspect somewhere along the initial programing, your programmers made the switch wrong or bad or full of guilt. Maybe they didn't fully understand the importance of being turned on, so they forgot to mention it to you.

It doesn't matter where you got your ideas and opinions of sex, and there's no need to go back and blame anyone for misinformation.

What matters now is that you have a choice. You can choose to embrace your design or not.

Use the switch, set it to ON, and dive into your own ecstasy.

Allowing yourself to be turned on, to be sexy, and to enjoy your sex is a direct pathway to a more spectacular, ecstatic, enlightened way of living.

The moment of orgasm is direct connection to Source, Universe, God. It's a reboot and a charging station all packed into one blissful expression of YES.

Have you ever noticed a person who is fully aware of their own sexy powers? It almost feels intoxicating to be around them. The air in the room feels charged, and their own excitement is contagious.

Imagine if we could all approach life with this super power intact?

All you have to do to access this place is to allow yourself to be turned on. Allow yourself to enjoy your own beautiful creation just because you want to.

If this is an area you struggle with, its perfectly understandable; most of the world struggles with understanding the true importance of sex. I'm simply offering you a different perspective—a wild card for you to use in the playing of your game.

If you let yourself be turned on by life, then life will give you many more experiences that will turn you on.

When You're On, You're On

When you understand that your sexuality is 100% about you, you will learn to lighten up and not put so much pressure on others to please you. It is no one's job to satisfy you.

We can expand this concept into all parts of life. Your life is 100% up to you, and you are the only one who can live it. It is up to you to allow for inspiration, desire, energy, excitement. It is up to you to embrace the gorgeous creature you are and to love every inch of yourself. It is up to you to get excited about life and to create beautiful and amazing things. It is up to you to learn more about yourself. It is up to you to flip your switch to ON and to feel your own energy coursing through your veins.

When you get to the place where you can boldly accept your own personal strength and beauty, then you will be able to see this beauty and strength radiating from everyone around you.

Have a love affair with yourself; let yourself be turned on and watch the response you get from the world around you. Others will be curious about the energy you exude. They will want a bit of what you have. The trick is you have to get it first.

Chapter 10
Contrast

I learned this lesson from Ester Hicks and her teachings from Abraham.

Contrast is a necessary part of our creation, because in the experiencing of what we don't want, we simultaneously get clear about what we do want. Having clarity around the things we do want will give us a focal point. Our laser focus on any one topic/subject/or thing will bring it into our experience. My understanding of this concept has helped me to shift my perspective and to give intense and deliberate thought to the things I wish to experience.

The trick to using this process is to start where you are and to be honest.

The first step is to write down in great detail all the things you do not want in your life.

I created several lists: one for relationships, one for my physical body, and one for work. I created a separate list for fun, family, money, travel, writing, inspiration, and art. The possibilities are endless.

The second step is to take some time with each list. This allowed me to distinguish the actual things I want to experience. Then, I wrote down the things I want to experience.

The next step is to get busy only paying attention to the things I want to feel and completely ignoring the things I do not want.

I throw the list of "do not wants" into the trash and just focus on the "do wants."

I got busy being happy and busy moving towards the things and feelings I want with laser focus.

I'll give an example about writing.

I was experiencing many days of not having words to write, a sort of writer's block. After getting clear about the feelings and sensations I did not want, I was able to get clear about what I did want. Then I got busy doing something else that brought me joy. After a few days of paying no attention to the lack of inspiration for writing, the words started flowing again.

My list:

I do not want to feel blocked.

I do not want to write nonsense.

I do not want to feel like a loser.

I do not want to waste my time.

I do not want to stare at my laptop for endless hours trying to conjure up words.

I do not want to feel disconnected from inspiration.

I do not want to feel disconnected from my heart.

I do not want to look like an idiot.

I do not want to waste my time.

Flip the script!

I want to feel inspired.

I want to write and share meaningful information and inspiration and insights.

I want to feel like I am making a difference by sharing my insights.

I want to use every second of this precious time and make it the most amazing experience of a life filled with love and gratitude and satisfaction.

I want to feel connected to my heart, to spirit, to magic, to source.

I want to be an amazing human.

I want to cherish all my time on this planet.

I took the list of do's and focused on the feelings behind all the things I wanted. I let myself feel great about the words. I also allowed myself to ignore the don't wants and voila! Like magic, the things I wanted started to appear.

Another example:

Let's look at money and work.

I don't want to be controlled.

I don't want to have a time schedule.

I don't want to wear a mask.

I don't want to have to report to anyone.

I don't want to be around lots of people.

I don't want to waste my time.

I don't want to feel worthless.

I want to be a shining light.

I want to influence lots of people.

I want to be paid well for my time, work, energy.

I want to enjoy my freedom.

I want to write a best-seller.

I want freedom to do what I want when I want.

I want to be paid extremely well to do the things I love to do.

I want to travel in comfort and class.

By focusing on my wants, I have been able to create meaningful work that pays very well. I relish in my time spent creating beautiful art. The art is so engaging that time ceases, and I am whisked away into a world of color, freedom and pure enjoyment. When I finish, my experience is complete satisfaction and an excitement to create more.

Fun sidenote: I just returned from a fantastic girl's trip to the Florida Keys. Our fun time was spent in comfort and class, and I was able to create a beautiful painting simply because I wanted to.

Chapter 11
Pack Your Bags: You're Going on an Adventure

Travel Light

Use it up or give it away.

Our things are made to be used. If we are not using them, then give them to someone who will.

Gifting of our precious things allows for a fun feeling of giving and receiving.

All of life is about giving and receiving.

Breathing is an act of giving and receiving.

Inhale to receive life's Prana.

Exhale to give it back to the universe.

Letting go of the things that hold you down, that clutter your space, will allow for an experience of lightness.

In my experience of travel, I have found that I only use a few of the things I actually pack. This has made me aware of the fact that I don't really need many things in order to enjoy my trip.

I see life like one big vacation: we come here to experience the grandeur of existence, and then we go home. If we travel light, then we open ourselves up for spontaneity and creativity. (Most of my travel outfits fit into these categories.)

Having fun with minimal things allows us to be innovative.

I've watched my mother do this over the years, and her creations are ingenious. If she doesn't have something she needs, she finds a way to create it. She is amazing with duct tape.

Her simple life has inspired me to want to use up what I have, to clear space and to invent new ways of doing things.

Believe it or not, one of my greatest moments in life was walking away from our giant 10k-sq-foot home with only some of my books and clothing. Letting that life go, letting the things go, and living from a suitcase may be extreme for most people, but for me, it was exhilarating.

Your Map

Now that you understand the things you focus on will become your reality, and now that you know how to get clear about distinguishing the things you want, it is time to write them down. Use these statements as a map for your journey and refer to mine often. I keep mine on a 3" x 5" card in my wallet; I call it my top five (physical, financial, social, mental, spiritual). I have given each area of my life a mission statement, and I live as if every word and experience is already a reality.

Fun little side note: I wrote this card about 10 years ago, and I'm happy to report that everything I wrote about I am now currently enjoying. Time to write a new card!

My Personal Top 5

1) I am so grateful for having a beautiful dancer's body. I am long, lean, strong, swift, flexible and smooth. My body is ready for anything: modeling, dance, aerial play, competition, performance, sports, fun.

2) I am so grateful for having several successful businesses, making me plenty of money. I am paid well and have more than enough to enjoy all of life's luxuries.

3) I am so grateful for having fun, freedom, family, friends, so much love and laughter, connection. I have the freedom to enjoy the people who are most important to me. I love openly and share. I am loved and supported, respected and appreciated as I love, appreciate, support and respect others.

4) I am so grateful for being multitalented and well educated. I love learning and am happy to learn something new each day. I love challenging my mind and pushing my limits.

5) I am so grateful for the experience of peace of mind. I owe no one. I help out when I choose. I am a blessing to those around me by being generous with my time, money and love. I am an inspiration of living a wholehearted life connected to spirit.

When I wrote out these words 10 years ago, I had no idea that life would throw me into the spin cycle of the cosmic washing machine. The life that had to be lived because of the turbulence has allowed me to filter out, clear away and let go of so much excessive nonsense. I know now what is truly important, and I remind myself to remember who I am and what I want to experience. I refer to my top 5 many times throughout each month.

Your Tools

<u>Pay attention</u> to the life you are already living. Open up to your true self and feel your connection to all of life.

The way you view life is completely up to you, and it can be changed if you choose to. You change it by gaining <u>perspective</u>. Using this tool will remind you take a step back and to see what is really going on in the big picture of your life.

You then get to <u>question your beliefs</u> about anything and everything by being <u>honest, facing your fear, and appreciating your time.</u>

Being gentle with yourself and cultivating a deep <u>love for yourself</u> will allow you to <u>use your body</u> to be present and to open your channels of <u>intuition.</u>

The more open you become, the more <u>creativity</u> you will experience. Your <u>imagination</u> will give you access to new and amazing <u>talents</u> and creations.

As you move through your journey and share your findings, you will see that the things you are <u>learning</u>

will become more solid for you as you <u>teach</u> them. You will openly <u>learn from every person and experience</u> and circumstance as you try <u>new things</u> along the way.

You will find so much <u>fun in the process</u>, enjoying all the <u>work</u> you do by being <u>playful.</u>

<u>Turning yourself on</u> with all the splendor inside you will light your path.

And finally, understanding that <u>contrast</u> is a part of this world will help you get even clearer about what you truly want to experience.

You are ready. It is time to allow for the adventure of your life to consume you. All you have is now, and now is perfect.

Chapter 12
Meditation

Meditations for Your Practice

Meditation is the act of getting quiet, relaxing your body and tapping into the universe.

It's like plugging yourself into an outlet and recharging your battery.

It is a useful tool for every part of your life, and it is so simple to access.

You can take as much time or as little time as you choose; it doesn't have to be a huge event. It is simply about setting an intention and quieting down.

With practice, you will find that you will be able to access this state throughout your day while walking, driving, exercising, waiting in line, washing the dishes, etc.

The details~

Breath

The common thread for all your meditations will be your breath.

Your mind needs something to focus on, so you will give it a job.

Let your breath move fully into your belly, filling your lungs completely. Then let all the breath move out of your lungs. You belly will rise and fall with each inhale and exhale. Follow the breath with your mind.

Thoughts

Your thoughts will want to consume you; it's ok and natural. When you find yourself thinking, gently bring your awareness back to your breath.

Focus on your breathing. I imagine thoughts are like clouds in the sky; pay no attention to them and they will just float on by. Focus on your breathing.

Body

Your body will want to twitch and move; you may even notice strange tickles and the urge to scratch and wiggle. All this is ok; be patient. It takes practice to allow for the body to relax completely.

I like to allow my mind to gently move through the body when I first begin my meditation. I move through all the toes and fingers and arms and legs, asking them to relax.

I let myself feel heavy. If you start at your feet, you can move up through all of the body with your imagination and allow each part to relax.

It feels like slipping into a warm bath. If you need to move or scratch or wiggle, then let it be ok and just come back to your breathing.

Time

If you set a timer, your mind will not be preoccupied with time, and you can dive into your quiet, relaxed state, knowing there will be an end. Start with just 5 minutes. After some practice, you can add time. Fifteen minutes seems to be the perfect amount of time for me. This will be completely up to you. Play around with your time limits.

Walking meditation

It is possible to access a deep meditative state with your eyes open and your body moving.

I use this when I'm driving or working out, walking, dancing, creating art or doing chores.

The possibilities are endless.

When you choose to try this type of meditation, you will also practice being hyper-focused on the task at hand. While the body goes through its motions, you will simultaneously watch it.

Set your intention to be focused on the task. Notice all the things that happen within the task. This will allow you to be completely involved in what you are doing; you may even lose track of time.

The thread is your breath; watch your breathing.

Always come back to your breath.

The Doorway and the Garden

My first experience

I was first introduced to a guided meditation when I was 12 years old. The memory of moving into this place is still present and clear in my mind.

I recommend setting some time and space for this meditation; 10 minutes will do. You will need a quiet room where you won't be interrupted, and you can lay down and relax completely. Silence is best, but if you find there are noises around you, soft music in the back ground or white noise will help you to ignore the noise.

Breathe.

Allow your mind to follow the breath.

Notice the inhale and exhale.

Feel your body getting more and more relaxed with each breath.

When thoughts pop into your mind, pay no attention.

Continue to watch your breathing and allow your muscles to soften.

Let your face relax and your arms get heavy.

Imagine you are slipping into a warm bath of water and floating effortlessly.

After some time, you will imagine a giant door.

Walk up to this door and open it.

Behind the door is a stairwell. You will walk down these steps taking your time to breathe with each step. Your body becomes more relaxed with each step.

At the bottom of the steps, you will see an entrance to a secret garden.

Imagine walking into this garden and smelling the fragrant flowers.

You hear the sound of a waterfall and walk towards it following a path that leads you there.

Next to the waterfall is a bench; you will take a seat at the bench.

Relax on this bench for a while, noticing all the beauty within this garden.

Listen to the sound of the water.

Then imagine someone you love, someone here or on the other side.

Invite them to join you on the bench.

Have a conversation with them.

After your conversation with them, thank your visitor and make your way out of the garden.

Follow the path, climb the stairs and walk through the door back into your present body.

Welcome back.

I use this exact meditation to talk to my daughter.

Sidenote: As I wrote this to you and re-read my words, I had an intense feeling of *déjà vu*.

These meditations are not set in any particular order; just pick one that resonates with you and give it a go.

Make sure to have a notebook handy and write down any thoughts you may have afterwards.

Meditation: How Did I Get Here?

Today, you will ask about your own creation.

This is a powerful, amazing, connecting meditation and an opportunity to know for yourself who you are and why you are here.

Asking the question alone in powerful. Now you will ask and get quiet and receive. Listen, feel, imagine, open up.

You will use the breathing technique I mentioned before. Notice your inhale and exhale. Giving your mind something to do will allow for your body to relax.

As your body relaxes, focus your mind inside your beating heart.

Feel every beat; feel the pulsing of the blood through your veins.

Imagine your heart glowing; let the glow expand over your entire being. Continue to expand throughout your room then to the neighborhood, the city the country, then the whole world. Expand through space, stars and planets. Continue expanding until there is no more imagination to fill your understanding.

This edge is the void; this is where you will find your answer.

Ask your question and sit in the empty place for a bit. No pressure, just curiosity.

When you are ready, come back. Turn around and move from the void through space and the stars and planets until you see Earth; notice the beauty of the blue planet you get to live on. Come back into your body. Feel your breath, feel your limbs, stretch and wiggle, then open your eyes.

Welcome back! How was that?

Walking Meditation: Notice What You Notice

In this meditation, you will be taking yourself to a place alone—a coffee shop or a park, someplace in public. With a pen and paper, sit in a place where you can relax and not be disturbed for a few minutes.

Take a few deep breaths, and first sit with your eyes closed.

Then with eyes open, allow for a soft gaze, not focusing on anything you see.

Listen.

Notice what you hear. Just listen for a few minutes. Let your ears open, all while continuing to focus on your breath.

Let your senses become heightened.

Notice what you smell.

Notice how your skin picks up the surrounding air.

Now you will let your eyes see the world around you start with the things that are immediately in front of you; let your focus move in and out. See the light and shadow then pay attention to the colors. Finally, notice the people. Notice what you are seeing about the people.

After a few minutes, come back into the present moment with a couple deep breaths. Maybe stretch a bit.

You will see that even though you were in public and your eyes were open, it was possible to access a deep meditative state.

Meditation: Self-Love

In this meditation, you'll need a mirror.

Set a timer for 5 minutes. Stand in front of a mirror and gaze into your own eyes. Do your best to relax your face and body, but hold your gaze. Notice what thoughts immediately creep into your mind and ask, "Where can I bring more love?" Continue gazing and breathing; let your gaze soften and continue to look into your eyes. Try your best to calm the body and continue relaxing your face. Ask again, "Where can I bring more love?"

When the time is up, finish by thanking the image you see in the mirror, then write down any thoughts.

Take another 5 to 10 minutes and sit quietly with your eyes shut. Imagine the image you were just looking at and allow your heart to open and pour love all over this person.

This is a tough meditation. It may bring up deep feeling of sadness, but with practice, you will eventually be able to hold your own gaze and bring such a feeling of love and appreciation for the person you are seeing.

Meditation: Going Back in Time

Find a quiet place to either sit or lay down. Set a timer.

Allow yourself to relax and breathe. Use the same techniques as mentioned before. After a few minutes of relaxing, allow your mind to travel back in time. Move back to your earliest memory of yourself. Recreate the scene in your mind. See the room, the people, the event in as much detail as you can remember. See yourself in this situation and allow yourself to interact with the younger version of you. Offer a hug to this little person. Share love with your younger self. If the story is sad, offer comfort. If the story is fun, play awhile. Before you leave, offer to take your little self with you into your present life. Create a space in your heart where they can sit and watch your life.

Taking the time to go back and see the things that are still present in your memory is a great way to see into the things that may be challenging for you today. Offering love and understanding will allow you to see the past with eyes of perspective and acceptance. Rewriting your past stories will simultaneously rewrite your future ones. Remember, the stories we tell ourselves become the beliefs we hold. These beliefs create our reality. By going back in time, you can shift the story by adding love.

Meditation: Talent

This is a fun meditation to try when you are wanting to know more about the talents and desires you possess.

Set up your meditation the same as before with a chosen time limit and a place to relax. Use the techniques you like most to access your deep relaxed state. When you are ready, you will imagine a beautiful place: a beach or a mountain scape, some place you love. You will invite your younger self along with you. You will watch what your younger person is doing in this place. Let your imagination soar; anything is possible here, so allow this young version of you to go wild. Then join in on the fun.

Together, you will explore to your heart's content, letting the younger wild side of you lead the way.

This meditation will show you your truest desires. They developed when you were young and innocent and didn't know limitation. These desires are your seedlings of talent. Talent can be developed. Take these new thoughts into your present life and see how you can embody this wild child of yours.

Meditation: It's All Made Up

Everything is made up.

The world around us and within us is all made up. Every possibility and limitation, the cultures and beliefs and the perceptions of everything around us had an origin point. It came from somewhere. Where did it come from?

Why not be the one to make it up?

In this meditation, once you have attained your deep relaxed state, you will ask yourself about the origin of your beliefs.

Who made them up in the first place?

Give yourself permission to make something up—a theory, a language, a dance move, a recipe, a fantasy creature, a new song. The possibilities are limitless.

Meditation: Silence

Now that you have been practicing with visualizing and keeping an active mind in your meditations, you are ready to access the deepest of all meditations. The most profound place to go is into the silence.

In this meditation, you will let your mind relax along with your body. You will give it a vacation from thinking.

Remember, the trick to turning the mind in any direction is to give it a task to focus on.

It doesn't really turn off, but you can mute it for a bit.

I pretend I hit the mute button on the remote control.

As before, you will access your deep relaxed state by watching your breathing and letting your muscles soften.

Give your mind the task of following the breaths, and then hit mute. Let it count breaths quietly in the background. Now you move into total nothingness. You move into complete void. You dissolve.

Meditation Is Fun

Now that you have a few ideas of where to go with your meditations, you can create your own. Have fun with it and get creative.

Make time each day to get into a state of deep relaxation. Allow yourself to connect to the source of all creation. This is the best way to live a powerful and meaningful life of love and wonder and delight.

Now get busy!

The End and the Beginning

> "The end of all our exploring
> will be to arrive where we started
> and know the place for the first time."
>
> TS Elliot

Excerpt from *Sunn*

Believe it or not, I have always been fascinated with death. For as long as I can remember, I have been curious with the existence of an afterlife and how to connect with it.

As a young woman, I used to volunteer with hospice and would sit with the dying. I would hold their hands and rub lotion on their feet. I would brush their hair and listen to the stories of these people ready to leave our world. They would talk about all the people they loved and the moments they were proud of in their lives. They would also talk to unseen visitors who were there ready to escort them to the other side.

I believed deeply there is something waiting for us all, and when the time is right, we will simply move on to a better place.

One of the elderly gentlemen came to me in a dream the night he passed; he thanked me for my visits and said goodbye.

When my daughter made her transition, my fascination was no longer just a curiosity but now a desperate need for answers. I had to know. I had to communicate.

If she chose me to be her mother, then she must have known prior to her earthly existence that I was going to travel this journey in search of an explanation. Her life was going to mean something and her death was going to be a doorway for all of us to get information and comfort.

I asked for assistance daily. I wrote in my journals religiously. Writing became my solace and my connection.

My daughter found a way to inspire my mind with beautiful messages from beyond, sharing her love and wisdom with me, and now with you.

I have opened my journals and blog posts to you as an intimate expression of

my perspective as a mother in pain and now joy.

Excerpt from *Year Two*

I am in my second year of grieving the death of my 19-year-old daughter. Her whirlwind of a life and her immediate and tragic death inspired me to keep a running log of my experience. I write down everything. I have filled 8 journals with my daily experiences and thoughts. I write to my daughter constantly.

She and I have a special way of communicating, and I am so thrilled to develop my ability more clearly.

I have been practicing daily. My early mornings are reserved for quiet contemplation, meditation and communication. I don't hear from her every day. In fact, many weeks go by without any communication, but when it comes, it floods in. She shows up in my dreams many nights. I hear her words in my thoughts and feel inspired to write them down. Later, I re-read the words and am always amazed at what comes through. I find symbols when I most need them. I hear random songs when I'm thinking of her. I have opened up my entire life to being more clearly connected to spirit and intuition. I know it is possible; I just need a lot of practice.

I have also realized that by writing, I have been able to take the stories out of my being and shelve them somewhere safe. I can open my mind to new information by letting go of the old stuff. Now when I tell a story, it is usually something that I have already written down in the moment and the retelling feels powerful. The emotion, which is still very present, occasionally triggers me, but as the days move on, I too am able to move on into a new and profound place.

Everything is a miracle.

Author's Bio

Sariah Ellsmore is first and foremost a Mother of four and a lover of life.

She's an entrepreneur as both the owner of SE School of Movement and co-owner of CrossFit Pagosa and a modern day renaissance woman who played roller derby under the name Whiplash, a helicopter pilot, aerial dancer, author and artist.

Sariah studied at Utah State University, Pacific School of Massage and Palm Beach Helicopters and enjoys spending time with her grown children, learning, traveling, flying, aerial art, performing, painting, and the great outdoors.

Residing in both Southern Colorado and South Florida, she has challenged herself to write daily after the death of one of her daughters. The result of this challenge is three books within three years all released by the death date.

She shares her personal journey of death, loss, grief and now love and inspiration as a way of honoring her daughter who passed.

You can connect with Sariah through social media

FaceBook sariah.ellsmore

Instagram sariahdance

Her Books are available on Amazon

SUNN

Year Two

www.ingramcontent.com/pod-product-compliance
Lightning Source LLC
Chambersburg PA
CBHW060818050426
42449CB00008B/1712